Concentration and Focus

The Oxford Centre for the Mind:

Short Courses

Gary Lorrison

Concentration and Focus

The Oxford Centre for the Mind

Short Courses

Powerful techniques to help you establish and maintain total concentration and mental focus.

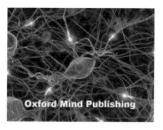

Gary Lorrison

Oxford Mind Publishing

THE OXFORD CENTRE FOR THE MIND LIMITED

#123,
94, London Road
Headington
Oxford OX3 9FN

email: info@oxfordmind.co.uk
web: www.oxfordmind.co.uk

Oxford Mind Publishing is a division of the Oxford Centre for the Mind Limited.

ISBN-13: 978-1490908489

ISBN-10: 149090848X

About the Author

Having studied law at Cambridge, Gary Lorrison started off his career working in London as a solicitor but quickly saw the light and left the legal profession to develop his interest in the mind. He quickly earned two degrees in philosophy but found himself focusing on how one could use the techniques of philosophy, psychology and science to run one's mind more effectively.

Since 2003, he has been actively involved in running personal development training programmes to help people improve their mental performance. He has a special interest in memory training and other ways of helping people absorb information as well as the techniques of logical, critical and analytical thinking and the limits of human rationality.

In his spare time he enjoys walking in the countryside, takes a keen interest in music playing a number of instruments and is an occasional skydiver.

He lives on a farm near Oxford with four dogs, three cats, three ducks, six geese, about five hundred sheep and the occasional human being.

Testimonials

Testimonials for our seminars: -

"Excellent - best course I have been on in ages - thought provoking and insightful"

"Great workshop. Coach created a very relaxing, easy and open atmosphere. Coach was helpful and had a very pleasant way of interacting with us"

"I am very happy I came to this workshop. It was good value for money and provided very useful skills that I know will help my studies"

"It's a great course - I would recommend you go on it"

"Good fun and value for money"

"Do it! - Very interesting and a good approach to de-stressing about work levels etc."

"It really works, especially the visualisation techniques"

For information on all of the courses run by the Oxford Centre for the Mind please visit our website:

www.oxfordmind.co.uk

Contents

ONE

INTRODUCTION

Aim

This course is designed to hone your ability to focus your mind and to be able to concentrate completely on one concept, one idea at a time. In many ways this is one of the most important and fundamental of all our mind mastery courses as it will help to lay a solid foundation for all of our other courses.

To focus your mind completely on one idea may sound easy, but, in fact, it is very difficult and a quick exercise we will ask you to do shortly will demonstrate that. Successfully learning to concentrate will benefit you immensely, both in taking control of your mind and in your wider life.

You will derive the direct benefits of being able to direct all of your concentration, and hence all of your energies, to a specific task, without letting yourself be distracted by trivia, and without letting your mind wander off without noticing. Imagine how much time you could save if you knew that all your mental energies could be directed toward a specific task until you have completed it, without any distraction getting in the way.

Exercise: The Benefits of Being Totally Focused

So that you can get an idea of the benefits of being able fully to concentrate on a single idea, we suggest that you now do this exercise. You will need a pen and paper for this.

Spend a few minutes thinking about a normal day at work or at home or studying, or whatever else you normally do during the day. Think of all the times you have been distracted from the task in hand, or how your mind has wandered off the subject, or having been interrupted you completely lose the thread of what you have been doing, or completely forgotten what you are doing. Spend five minutes brainstorming and writing down all the times you can think of.

When you have done that, think about how much better it would be if you could eliminate all of those distractions and bring all your attention to the task in hand. Think about how you would feel as a result, how much time you might save, what else you could do with that time, and what effects that might have on your life. Note these benefits down. We are going to use these benefits to help you start and continue with this concentration course.

The Benefits of Good Concentration

In addition to the direct benefits of good concentration, there are other beneficial side effects. The process by which you will learn to concentrate causes both your mind and your body to relax, and yet to be alert at the same time - technically this is known as an *alpha* state. Being able to achieve this state of relaxed alertness will positively impact on all areas of mental performance and can also be utilised to improve your general physical performance. For instance, people who perform great feats of memory, speed reading, creativity, or calculation are often in an *alpha* state, and being in the even more relaxed *theta* state is associated with bursts of great inspiration or insight. The notes of men of genius, such as Einstein and Mozart, suggest that they were in such states of mind during their moments of great creativity.

If you ever watch a top class athlete preparing for a race you might see that they perform certain exercises designed to help them focus on their event. They are attempting to achieve a similar mental state. One of the additional benefits of being in this relaxed state is an improvement in reaction times. Generally, reaction times for someone in an *alpha* state fall from 0.5 seconds to 0.3 seconds – not much, but particularly important in some sports such as sprinting or motor racing, and possibly the difference between success and failure, or even life and death.

There are other physical benefits. These include a reduction in the rate at which your body requires oxygen – this may fall by up to twenty per cent. As a result of this your heart rate and rate of respiration fall, putting less strain on your heart and reducing the production of carbon dioxide. The upshot of this is that your body undergoes a significant reduction in physical stress.

Associated with this is a reduction in mental stress. You may have identified stress as one of the factors leading to poor concentration in the exercise you have just done. By being able to focus your mind completely on one thing, you will eliminate the factors that cause mental stress. If you think about it for a moment, most, if not all, of the things that cause us to become stressed, anxious or depressed are either rooted in the past or in the future. By focusing fully on one idea you eliminate any thoughts about the past or future, and therefore eliminate anxiety and stress. This is not to say that you ignore problems, but instead that you will be able to deal with them when you want to, and not be at the mercy of your worries.

Exercise: Identifying the Causes of Anxiety and Stress

Take a few moments to identify all of the things that cause you to become stressed, anxious or depressed, and note them down.

When you have done that, try to identify which are rooted in the past, which in the immediate present, and which are in the future.

How many were in the immediate present? In all likelihood very few. Most of the things we worry about are either related to things that are going to happen to us in the future, or as a result of things that have happened to us in the past. So, if you can learn to focus your concentration completely on what you are doing and in the present moment, you will find that your mental stress is greatly reduced or even eliminated.

The Benefits of Reducing or Eliminating Stress

You will find that by eliminating mental stress, you will reduce your physical stress too. Since the brain and the body are ultimately both part of the same physiological system, benefits in one area will often lead to benefits in another area. You may find that your muscular tension reduces, leading to various other beneficial health effects.

If you find that you are still carrying physical tension in your body after learning to concentrate, investigate exercise classes aimed at increasing your flexibility and reducing physical tension such as yoga.

You will also find that, because proper concentration allows your mind to go into a state of relaxed alertness, and because this leads to a reduction in bodily and mental tension, your ability to relax will soar. When you have become reasonably adept at doing the concentration exercises, you might find that you are as relaxed after twenty minutes concentration as you are after a good night's sleep. You may be able to manage with less sleep, and yet still feel full energy, enabling you to get much more out of your life.

This is a Practical Course
Remember as you go through this course that it is designed to be practical, not theoretical. You should do all of the exercises when we indicate. If you just read through the course without doing any of the exercises, you might gain an intellectual understanding of what the course is about, but you will not gain the benefits you will from actively participating.

Onword
Having now explained the benefits of this course, we will now look more closely at just what we mean by concentration and what you will be doing to develop it.

TWO

WHAT IS CONCENTRATION?

In this course we treat concentration as meaning being completely focused on one idea at a time, with the whole of your mind, and being able to maintain complete focus on that one idea for an extended period of time. You will be completely and totally absorbed in that one idea to the exclusion of all others.

Concentration is *being* - being in the present moment and being completely oblivious to the past and the future. You might have achieved this state at certain times in your life. For instance, whenever you have focused entirely on something that you were doing, and lost yourself in it so much that you completely lost track of time and the world around you, you will have been in a concentrated state of mind.

Exercise: Identifying Moments of Pure Concentration
Spend a few moments allowing yourself to become completely relaxed and review your life to date. Try to identify times in your life when you have been completely absorbed in one thing and completely lost yourself in it. It might be a time that you were engaged in a hobby, or a sport, reading a book, taking a walk or making love. Close your eyes and try to remember what it felt like. See if you can feel now what it felt like then. This is the state of mind that we want you to achieve on a consistent basis.

If you want to make any notes feel free to do so.

You may think from the description above that it is very easy to achieve this concentrated mental state. In fact, for most people it is very difficult and to achieve it on a consistent basis requires constant, regular practice.

Exercise: the Difficulties of Maintaining Concentration

In this exercise you will see how good you are at concentrating and how difficult it can be to consistently hold one idea in your mind.

You will need a quiet environment where you are unlikely to be disturbed for a few minutes, a pen and paper and a timer of some sort that has an alarm.

In this exercise you are going to close your eyes and think of an everyday object - an apple - for just five minutes. You are going to imagine what it looks like and hold that image in your mind's eye to the exclusion of all else for just five minutes. Use the alarm to alert you when the five minutes are up.

If, during this five-minute period, you notice your thoughts wandering, make a mark on the paper, without opening your eyes, and calmly redirect your mind to the image of the apple. If your mind wanders again, make another mark. Every time your mind wanders during this period, make a mark and calmly redirect your mind to the image of the apple. If you find yourself checking before the five minutes are up, make another mark - because you will be thinking of the time that has elapsed and not the apple.

When you have finished take a look at the number of marks you have made. Does it accurately reflect how many times your mind wandered? You may find that you got so engrossed in a new train of thought that you didn't even notice your mind wandering, and failed to record it.

If you have made no marks, and your mind truly did not wander at all, congratulations! You are able to achieve something that very few people are able – total and complete concentration.

In all likelihood, you were probably only able to hold the image of the apple for a few seconds before your mind started wandering. Do not worry about that. That is what most people experience and is entirely natural.

We suggest that you now review the exercise you have just done. Record what you experienced and your reaction to it in your notes.

Fortunately, even if you did find the last exercise surprisingly difficult, you will be pleased to know that with practice you can develop your ability to concentrate. The concentration exercises that you will be taught are easy to learn, only take a short amount of time each day, and are very enjoyable and relaxing.

Onword

In the following section we will show you how to approach the concentration exercises and then following on from that the specific concentration exercises that we use in this course.

THREE

PREPARING FOR CONCENTRATION

In this section we outline various matters that you should pay attention to before you start any of the concentration exercises we will be outlining in the following sections.

Before You Start

To ensure that you gain the most from your concentration exercises, it is essential that you are properly prepared. You should pay attention to the following factors before you begin: -

Time

You will need to set aside twenty to thirty minutes when you are unlikely to be disturbed by anyone else.

Environment

Choose a place to do your concentration exercise that is quiet, clean and pleasant. It should be somewhere that you will feel comfortable, that you will want to return to, and somewhere that you won't be disturbed.

If possible, use a separate room, or mark off a part of a room that you can devote solely to these exercises. You might wish to light scented candles. Do whatever it takes to create a pleasant atmosphere that works for you.

If you want to, you can do these exercises outside in the open air, provided that there are no distractions. If you live in the countryside or by the sea, or anywhere where there is a pleasant outdoor environment, this would be an excellent alternative.

Make sure that you do your exercises where it is not too bright. If you are indoors, shut the curtains, and dim the lights. If you are outside, try to choose a time of day when the sun is not too bright, or stay in the shade.

Your Physical State

To gain best results, you should be free of all physical distractions: muscular tension, itches and so on. Any physical discomfort, tension or stress is likely to distract you and you should do whatever you can to reduce or eliminate it before you start.

The best way of reducing physical tension is to follow a some kind of exercise regime which raises your heart rate for an extended period of time. Exercises which stretch your muscles and increase your flexibility will help reduce physical tension

Clothing

Make sure that you are wearing comfortable, warm, loose clothing: no shoes, but socks are okay. Make sure that you aren't wearing anything tight that is likely to cause discomfort, as you will be sitting still for some time.

You may wish to have a blanket handy as your body temperature is likely to drop as you relax.

Posture

You will do the concentration exercises in a sitting position. Your ultimate aim will be to achieve the concentrated state of mind in *any* situation, but while you are learning, to make it as easy as possible for you we ask that you sit down in the most comfortable manner possible.

You can either sit in a chair or on the floor. If you decide to use a chair, try and use one with a straight, hard back. This will help keep your back straight and prevent you from slouching. You knees should not be too bent - they should be at an angle greater than 90 degrees (that means that your feet should be further away than your knees from your chair). Rest your hands in your lap or wherever they feel most comfortable.

If you would rather sit on the floor, you can sit either cross-legged, or in the lotus position. If you find it difficult to sit like this, try sitting with your back against a wall or with a cushion under your backside. Again rest your hands in your lap in whatever way feels comfortable.

Whichever way you decide to sit, concentrate on keeping your back straight and your head well balanced. Make sure that you are sitting on your sitting bone, located under your buttocks, and not slouched at all. This will ensure that your body is balanced, that your muscles are relaxed and that any physical tension is minimised. You should be as comfortable as you possibly can.

Diet

Make sure that you eat healthily before the first time you practise and avoid alcohol and any kind of drugs for twenty-four hours beforehand if at all possible.

Avoid doing the concentration exercises within one hour of eating.

Phone

Take the phone off the hook or turn it off, so that you will not be disturbed.

Family

Make sure your family or other household members know that you would like to have this period of time to yourself and do not want to be disturbed. If they want to join in with you, that is perfectly acceptable, and doing these exercises in a group can be fun.

Music

We suggest that, initially, you do these exercises in silence, just to get a sense of how it feels to do so. You may, though, eventually, want to do them with music or other relaxing sounds playing in the background. If you do the exercises in an outdoor environment, you may well hear some natural sounds such as birdsong, wind or animal noises anyway and you should not find these distracting.

If you do use your own music, make sure that what you choose is conducive to relaxation. Led Zeppelin's music may be great, but it is unlikely to help your reach a relaxed state of mind!

Certain types of music are very good for helping still the mind, inducing an *alpha* state, and harmonizing mind and body. Classical music from the Baroque period, particularly Bach, is effective, as is music by Mozart, Telemann and Handel. The aim of the composers in this period was to create compositions of a harmonious whole, and the result of this is music which is ideal for achieving a relaxed state of mind.

Alternatively, you might like to try Indian classical music, the aim of which is to encourage certain moods. You will find if you listen to this kind of music, it doesn't appear to progress with time in the same way that much western music does (western music always seems to be *going* somewhere), but rather creates a mood or landscape for the ears in which the process of time progressing is not obvious. Perhaps this says something interesting about the difference between eastern and western cultures.

Other recordings you might like to try are sounds of waves breaking against the shore, which is very relaxing, or birdsong. In fact, you can use anything that helps you attain a relaxed state of mind without distracting you.

Timer

Initially, we suggest you do the exercises for twenty minutes at a time. You may lose track of time while you are doing them, so make sure that you have some way of knowing when your time is up, such as an alarm clock. As you progress, you might like to extend the time that you spend in a concentrated state of mind. You may find that when you have decided how long you want to spend, your inner body clock will let you know when your time is up with a surprising degree of accuracy.

Paper and Pen

When you have finished, you might find it beneficial to make a note of your experiences and how the exercises went for you, so have a pen and paper handy. You may want to use a notebook or journal so that you can keep all your notes together in one place.

Now You are Ready!

Once you are properly prepared you can begin the concentration exercises. There are three different styles of concentration exercise to choose from. There are many other styles, but three is sufficient for our purposes. The next section covers these in detail.

FOUR

THE CONCENTRATION EXERCISES

In this section we outline a number of different concentration styles and explain how specifically to do the concentration exercises. We identify certain obstacles to concentration, how to overcome them and explain what to do when you have finished your concentration exercises.

How to do the Concentration Exercises

In this section, you are going to learn three different styles of concentration exercise. With each different style you will use a particular idea or *hook* to focus on. What the hook is doesn't really matter. Each is merely a device to help you focus the mind.

We suggest that you adopt the following approach for familiarising yourself with the three different styles. Pick the first of the three styles and do it at least once a day every day for one week. At the end of this week, move on to the second style and then do that every day for a week. Repeat this with the third style.

When you have experienced all three for a sufficient period of time, we suggest you select the one that you find works best for you and stay with it. Once you have done so, you should not need to change again, unless you have a specific reason to (for example, if you want to benefits to the eyes that the candle exercise brings).

When you have read through the section concerning the style you are going to try, move on to the chapter *'Concentration in practice'*, which will explain precisely how to put the concentration exercises into practice.

Style 1: Focusing on Breathing and Counting

This exercise is the most simple of the three. However, just because it is simple does not mean that it is any less effective. It is just as good as the other two exercises. The only problem that you may have is that you may find it too simple. But if, after having tried it and the other two exercises, you find that you are happy with this one, stay with it.

In this exercise you will focus completely on your breath as it enters and leaves your body and count each breath. Breathe in slowly through your nose for three seconds. Focus on the feel of your breath as it enters your nose. Breathe deeply so that your abdomen fills with air. Hold it for three seconds and then breathe out slowly for another three seconds. Again, focus on the feel of the air as it streams out through your nose.

Count each breath. Count one for the first breath, two for the second, three for the third and four for the fourth. When you have reached four, go back to the beginning and start again at one. Throughout this exercise, you will be counting from one to four as you breathe.

This is the complete exercise. It is very simple but also very effective. Initially do it for twenty minutes. As you become more proficient, and you find your ability to focus increasing, you may want to extend this time.

Style 2: Focusing on a Repeated Word or Phrase

In this exercise, you will use a repeated word or phrase to focus on. We will call this your *concentration word*.

What is a Concentration Word?

A concentration word is simply a word or phrase which you will use as a convenient idea to focus on. In theory, the actual word or phrase you use is unimportant and could be anything, as it is merely a device to focus the attention. However, in practice, if you adopt this exercise as your long-term concentration exercise, the word or phrase that you choose may take on a special meaning and importance for you.

Selecting your Concentration Word

Concentration words are also known as mantras. Many mantras have religious connotations. For instance, in the Roman Catholic tradition, the repetition of the *Lord's Prayer* has the form of a mantra; in Hinduism many mantras are used, the best known of which is the Sanskrit word *Om*. However, as far as you are concerned there is no need for the word or phrase you adopt to have any religious nature. Words such as 'calm', 'peace', or 'relax' will work just as well. Unless you have a good reason not to, we suggest that you pick one of these.

SELECT YOUR CONCENTRATION WORD NOW.

If you feel the need, make a written note of it.

Once you have selected your concentration word there is no reason for you ever to change it, so stay with it. Also, since it may take on a special meaning for you over time, we suggest that you keep it private and don't tell anyone else what it is.

How to Use the Concentration Word

To focus with your concentration word, breathe in the same way as you did for the previous breathing exercise. Once you have got your breathing rhythm established, start to hear the concentration word emanate from inside your head. Let it come naturally. Do not force it. If you want to, and if you will find it easier to concentrate, feel free to say it out loud, being careful to ensure that it won't disturb anyone else. Say your concentration word once per breath. The rhythm should suggest itself naturally to you.

At the same time, with your eyes closed, focus on the area immediately behind the bridge of your nose between your eyes. This area corresponds to your hypothalamus, the region of your brain which controls your stress levels. By focusing on this area, you will be able to relax more easily.

As with the breathing exercise, initially do this exercise for a period of twenty minutes, increasing the duration when you feel you are ready.

Style 3: Focusing on a Candle

In this exercise you will use a candle as a point of visual focus. Unlike the other two exercises you will not be saying any words to yourself, and so you may find playing music in the background may be useful. This exercise has the additional benefit of stimulating the brain via the optic nerve, improving your eyesight, and strengthening the eye muscles.

How to do the Candle Exercise

Prepare and breathe in the same way as for the other two exercises. Set up the candle about three feet away from your eyes. Gaze at the flame for a minute or until tears start to fill your eyes. Then close your eyes and visualise the candle in your mind's eye. Keep your eyes closed until the image starts to fade. When it does, open your eyes again and repeat the process. Over time you will find that you can extend both the period that you can focus on the candle, and the period of visualisation with your eyes closed.

As with the other two exercises, start off doing it for twenty minutes, and when you feel you are ready, extend this period.

FIVE

CONCENTRATION IN PRACTICE

When you are ready to start, sit down in whichever manner you have chosen. Sit still for five minutes, and allow yourself to relax. Breathe deeply from your abdomen. Breathe in for a count of three, hold for another three count, and exhale for a count of three. Do not strain as you breathe.

How to Breathe Well

Having started to become aware of how you currently breathe, you may have noticed that you are not breathing deeply from the abdomen. Since this is the type of breath that you want to encourage it is important to know how to do it properly.

Abdominal Breathing

1. Place your fingers gently on your stomach an inch or so below the navel.

2. Inhale deeply, slowly and evenly through your nose. Feel your abdomen swell. Don't strain or allow your chest to rise. You want a natural effortless flow of breath.

3. Hold the breath for a few moments and then exhale slowly and evenly until you feel your abdomen fall.

4. Repeat this slow inhalation, followed by slow exhalation with no pauses.

5. Breathe in and out 5 times.

For a good deep breath that prioritises abdominal breathing there are three elements: -

The Inhalation

Here air is drawn into the lungs through the nose, filling up the abdomen, then the chest and up towards the neck

The Hold

The breath is held for a short period. This holding period allows the oxygen to permeate from the lungs into the bloodstream, ensuring that the body is fully oxygenated.

The Exhalation

Stale air is expelled from the lungs and toxins are eliminated from the body. By emptying the lungs fully, the potential is created for more fresh air to enter the lungs on the following breath. Contract your abdomen to force the air out.

When breathing in this manner, focus on your abdomen as you take air deeply in to your lungs. If you are still not sure that you are doing this correctly, try to make a noise similar to Darth Vader in your throat as you breathe. This will ensure that you are using your abdomen and not another part of your chest to draw air into your lungs.

When you have spent five minutes sitting like this, breathing deeply and relaxing, you should be ready to start your chosen concentration exercise.

Concentration

COMMAND YOUR MIND TO BE STILL

Now, sit quietly and spend the next twenty minutes doing whichever concentration exercise you have chosen to do. Initially limit yourself to twenty minutes. As you become more adept, you may want to extend the time that you spend in concentration.

Your aim is to keep relaxed and focus the whole of your mental attention completely and utterly on whichever mental hook you are using. If you are doing the breathing and counting exercise, focus completely on your breath and the count. If you are using a concentration word, focus entirely on that. If you are focusing on the candle, focus your attention entirely on that and nothing else. Initially, you may only be able to focus for a few seconds at a time before your mind wanders. As you continue with your practice, you will find that the period that you can keep your mind focused on your object of concentration will increase.

What You May Experience

As you do the concentration exercises, you may notice that you become more and more relaxed and that your breathing slows down. Your body temperature may fall slightly and so you may feel a little cold. This is why we suggest that you have a blanket to hand. You may also notice that your body starts to feel heavy, particularly your hands and feet. This is natural and nothing to worry about. It merely indicates that you are indeed relaxing properly.

Overall you should find the experience very enjoyable and relaxing.

Obstacles to Concentration

You may experience some of the following problems during your concentration practice: -

Distraction

The main obstacle to concentration you are likely to come across is one of distraction. You will undoubtedly find your thoughts wandering away from your object of concentration, and when this happens you will probably even fail to notice that your thoughts have wandered. Do not worry about this. Most people have this problem, particularly in the early stages. Having a lively mind is usually considered very important, but here we are trying to keep the mind still, so that you can focus on one thing at a time. By persevering, you will be able to extend the period for which you can maintain concentration.

When you become aware that your mind has wandered, and it may take some time before you notice that it has, calmly redirect it back to the object of focus. Imagine that your mental focus is like the groove in a record, and that you are trying to keep your attention concentrated in the groove, rather than letting it jump around. When you realise that your attention has wandered, do not allow yourself to become frustrated. Ensure that you stay relaxed. If you have to choose between maintaining concentration and being relaxed, choose relaxation.

Strange Thoughts

When your mind wanders, you may be surprised at some of the thoughts that you have. If you do have strange thoughts, do not worry. Just as you can have strange dreams when you are asleep, you can have strange thoughts when your mind is in a state of deep relaxation. It is perfectly natural. Just acknowledge these thoughts and calmly redirect your mind back to the object of focus.

Impatience

Another obstacle to success in your concentration exercises is impatience. In our society we want results quickly, and quite often will not tolerate anything that does not bring immediate results. You *will* notice immediate benefits from your concentration practice, but the benefits are cumulative, so to gain the full benefits of these concentration exercises you must persevere. We will say more about this in the ongoing practice section.

Anxiety

If you feel anxious while doing your concentration exercises, try and work out what the cause of the anxiety is. It may be physical. For instance, you may be physically tense and unable to relax. Deal with any other physical distractions as they occur, such as scratching an itch or blowing your nose. If you don't deal with them as they occur, they might end up becoming much more of a distraction.

It may be that you feel anxious for other reasons – work, financial, personal and so on. If that is the case and you really don't think that you will be able to concentrate successfully on a particular day, consider postponing the concentration element of the exercises either until later on in the day or to the following day. However, persevere with the relaxation elements of the exercises, as it will help to reduce your anxiety.

In the longer term, as you persevere with your concentration exercises, the occasions on which you are unable to concentrate through anxiety will become fewer and fewer. After all, one of the benefits of this course is to help reduce your stress levels and with less stress, there will be fewer things likely to distract you.

Finishing your Concentration Exercises

At the end of the period you have set aside for your concentration exercise gradually bring your focus back to the outside world. Imagine yourself crossing a threshold back to the outer world. You should feel extremely relaxed and in a very good mental state.

Try and stay relaxed as you come back into the world. We suggest that you keep a journal and make a brief note of your experiences each time you do the concentration exercises. Make a note of which style seems to work best for you, whether any particular time of day is better for you – whether you feel you prefer to have music or not and any other things that occur to you to write down. Do not censor yourself. In this relaxed state of mind you may have some interesting insights. If your mind wandered and you had any distracting thoughts, you might like to record these and think about what they mean to you.

Onword

In the following section, we will deal with some practical matters that will ensure that you obtain the full benefits from your concentration exercises.

SIX

ONGOING PRACTICE

Initial Stages

In the early stages of your concentration practice, ensure that you do the exercises every day for at least a month. By then you should be starting to get an idea of what it feels like to be in a state of concentration, and you may be have an idea which style you prefer.

When that month is up, assess what you have learnt and the benefits you have derived from doing the exercises and consider whether you want to continue. Write down what you think you have gained from doing these exercises and what benefits they have brought to you in your life. Write down anything else that occurs to you as well. Also note down what you think you will gain from continuing to do your concentration exercises and identify what would happen if you gave up. Use these notes as a source of motivation to continue with the exercises. We advise you to conduct a review of your progress every three months.

Ideally, you will want to incorporate the concentration exercises into your life on an ongoing daily basis. If you do so the benefits to your long-term mental and physical health will be maximised. With these exercises, success is not just a goal, it is also the path itself, and part of that success is the discipline that comes with ongoing perseverance. Therefore, you should never reach a point where you can think to yourself that you have mastered the discipline of concentration and can therefore stop the exercises.

As we have already said, one of the greatest obstacles to progress with these exercises is impatience. You will initially notice large benefits, but gradually the law of diminishing returns will set in, and the benefits will become less noticeable. However, the long term benefits are just as important even if they are less obvious. So make a decision to persevere.

Another danger is that you will acknowledge the benefits of concentration but fail to make a committed decision to do the exercises regularly. In this case, you will obtain some benefit and be able to relax whenever you do the exercises, but not obtain the long term benefits of being able to completely focus your mind. The rest of this section is aimed at helping you persist with your exercises.

Preferred Style

When you have been doing the exercises for a month, we suggest that you assess which of the three styles you prefer and continue using that style from then on. Remember that each style is merely a device for your mind, something to focus on, and so at a deeper level, it doesn't really matter which one you choose. But if you keep changing all the time, you will be sending a message to your subconscious that it need not stick with one idea, and the whole point of this course is to get to your mind to be able to do just that.

Time of Day

In the initial stages you might like to experiment with practising at different times of day. However, when you have identified the time of day that suits you best, try to stick with it. For most people the best times are either immediately after waking up or just before going to bed. If you choose the latter make sure you do not fall asleep while doing your exercises. You will find that these exercises will help you to sleep better anyway, as they will help you to eliminate distracting thoughts.

How Long?

You should spend about twenty minutes at a time performing your concentration exercises. If you cannot spare twenty minutes, do whatever you can, but consider rescheduling your other commitments. In the long run the benefits of spending twenty minutes a day doing these exercises will outweigh the costs. Try always to focus on the longer-term benefits. Most people's problems, difficulties and challenges usually spring from having a focus that is too short term.

If you have more time available, try to do two twenty-minute sessions a day, one in the morning, one in the evening. Doing two sessions a day will improve your long-term ability to concentrate. Alternatively, if you only have time to do one session, try to extend that session, aiming to increase it to forty minutes a day if you can. However, if you do not have the extra time, one twenty-minute session per day is perfectly acceptable.

Planning

An excellent way of making sure that you continue with your exercises is to plan your day in advance. Furthermore, if your plans are in writing you are more likely to put them into practice. The best time to do your planning is the night before, so that when you do are planning you are not distracted by the events of the following day. This makes it easier to be firm about what you are going to do.

Onword

In the following section we will deal with ways of taking the benefits you have obtained from doing the concentration exercises into your wider life.

SEVEN

LIFESTYLE CONSIDERATIONS

Some of the comments in this section may become more meaningful when you have been doing your concentration exercises for a number of weeks. By then you should be beginning to appreciate the benefits of having a focused mind, and the physical and mental benefits of a reduction in stress. You may be developing a more relaxed and philosophical outlook on life and be starting to feel much more in control of yourself.

Live in the Moment

Try to maintain a focused attitude to life at all times. Keep your attention fully on the present moment and on what you are doing right now. Do not be distracted by the past or the future. The past is gone and the future has not happened yet. Adopting this outlook will help you stay completely focused on whatever it is that you are doing at any particular time.

This does not mean, of course, that you should neglect planning for the future, or analysing the past. Planning for the future is an important activity, and by looking back to the past we can encounter pleasant memories as well as find things that we can learn from.

Instead, what you should do, either when planning for the future or analysing the past, is to focus completely on that task and on nothing else. You will do it better and in less time. At the same time try and maintain a peaceful and philosophical attitude to life. You have already discovered that it is very rare that your problems are in the present moment. They usually stem from things that have happened in the past, or from worries about the future. If you take that view, you may find that they become less important.

If you do change your outlook on life in this way, you may find that what you consider important to you changes. You may also find that you become more self-confident and that you start to stand out from the crowd as someone who is in control of their life, rather than at the mercy of events. Another benefit is that your new attitude may start to rub off on those around you, as we all have a natural tendency to imitate the people around us.

Concentration at Work

When you are at work, try to maintain the mental focus that we have advocated here. Do one task at a time, focus on it completely and if at all possible complete it before moving on to the next one. Sometimes this may be impossible as you may have a number of overlapping tasks. For instance, if you work in an office, you may have phones to answer, letters to write, meetings to attend and so on, such that you cannot finish one before going on to another. What you can still do, though, is to give each one your complete attention while you are doing it. So, for example, don't try to work on the computer while you are using the phone. You will do both tasks much better if you focus on each one at a time.

Another good habit you can adopt is to prioritise the bigger more important tasks and do them first (the ones we normally put off!). If so, you will find that they are not usually as bad as you had imagined they would be, and as a result of doing them, you will have less to worry about. If you have lots of small relatively unimportant tasks to do, try and do them all together in one go, after you have done your more important tasks. If possible, try and delegate the smaller tasks so that you can concentrate on what is important, and focus on your strengths.

When it is time for a break during your working day, refrain from bad habits such as having a coffee or a cigarette, or snacking on junk food. Instead, consider going outside, taking a few deep breaths and doing a mini-concentration session. You will find that doing this will have far greater beneficial effects in the long term than a smoke or a shot of caffeine. Alternatively, go outside for a walk. Keep your eyes open and unfocused. Breathe slowly and deeply. Relax. You will return to work motivated and full of energy.

Take Regular Walks

One of the best ways of adopting a focused and concentrated attitude to life is to go for regular walks. Going for a walk is a great way of getting away from your problems and a chance to think deeply without being distracted. It is also, of course, a great way of staying fit and healthy.

Whenever you are walking try to adopt a reflective, focused approach. Still your mind and try to stay as relaxed as possible. Synchronise your breathing with your footsteps and feel your breath as you inhale and exhale. Make sure you feel the ground firmly under your feet as you walk along. Hear the noises of nature, smell the smells and give your senses a feast. You will find this a most beneficial way of living.

Enhancing Your Long Term Attention Span

Select a task or project that you have to do or want to do. It could be anything such as reading a book, writing a letter, a hobby of some sort, or a business project. What it is doesn't matter, as long as it is something that can be done for an extended period of time, and can be repeated, so that you can measure how your attention span increases over time. Something that you can do regularly is therefore ideal.

Set an initial time period of two hours, and during this period give your selected task your total and complete attention. Do not allow anyone else to distract you. If necessary, tell your family, friends or colleagues that you do not wish to be disturbed during this period.

Before you start make sure that you have all the materials that you need, so that you will not have to interrupt your task while you are doing it. When you start, make sure that you give it your complete and undivided attention for the entire two-hour period. Do not allow anything to distract you until your two hours are up. If you find that your attention is wandering, calmly redirect your mind to the task at hand. Use the same mental approach that you use for your concentration exercises.

When you are able to go two hours without becoming distracted, gradually lengthen this time span in increments of half an hour at a time (so two hours, then two and half hours, then three hours and so on). Do not increase this time span until you are confident that you can go for the whole period without being distracted and with no fall off in performance.

Planning for Long Term Concentration

As with the concentration exercises, it is a good idea to plan how you intend to incorporate these long-term concentration exercises into your life.

Make a few notes about what you can do at home, at work and in other aspects of your life to adopt and maintain this attitude. Review these notes regularly (once every three months or so) to see if you are living up to your standards and constantly strive to improve.

Onword

You have now completed the concentration course. The following section deals with some final points.

EIGHT

AFTERWORD

Throughout this course we have used the terms concentration, focus and relaxation. Some of you who are familiar with meditation may have noticed that the exercises we have outlined here are essentially the same as certain meditation exercises.

We have adopted our terminology because the aims of this course are different from those of a meditation course where the objectives are more spiritual in nature. In this course, the aims and benefits are purely practical, although the methods are similar.

We have refrained from using the term meditation until now as for some people it might have religious connotations. In fact, meditation is merely concerned with stilling the mind in the same way we have outlined here. Some religions believe that meditation brings you certain spiritual benefits. Whether this is true or not, the benefits of doing the concentration exercises outlined in this course are available to everyone.

More Short Courses Coming Soon!

Visualisation

Analytical Thinking

Creative Thinking

Setting and Achieving Goals

Powerful States of Mind

Essential Communication Skills

Emulating Success

Healthy Eating

Healthy Sleep

Printed in Poland
by Amazon Fulfillment
Poland Sp. z o.o., Wrocław